New Bremen 2000

# New Bremen 2000

Photography by Robert Flischel
Text by Mark Bernstein

ORANGE FRAZER PRESS
Wilmington, Ohio USA
2000

ISBN 1-882203-66-6




Orange Frazer Press, Inc.
Box 214
37 ½ West Main Street
Wilmington, Ohio 45177

Telephone 1.800.852.9332 for price and shipping information
Web Site: www.orangefrazer.com
E-mail address: editor@orangefrazer.com

Library of Congress Cataloging-in-Publication Data

Flischel, Robert A.
    New Bremen 2000 / by Robert Flischel and Mark Bernstein.
        p. cm.
    ISBN 1-882203-66-6 (hardcover)
    1. New Bremen (Ohio)--Pictorial works. 2. New Bremen (Ohio)--Social life and
  customs. 3. New Bremen (Ohio)--Biography.  I. Bernstein Mark (Mark Douglas), 1950-
  II. Title.

F499.N37 F58 2000
977.1'43--dc21

                                                        00-044100

Printed in Canada

To the future generations of New Bremen
and German Township, who will inherit the images
of today and embrace them as their past.

# Acknowledgments

It takes a village to make a book. In the case of New Bremen 2000, we add a photographer and a writer, too. The award-winning Cincinnati photographer, Bob Flischel, had remembered New Bremen with affection from an earlier visit years ago. "I looked forward to going back. Everything about the town made me feel good. I can honestly say, now, that I've gone over every inch of this town. What impressed me the most was the openness, responsiveness, and friendliness to my photographic adventures. Afterwards, I felt like an old familiar friend." Bob took hundreds and hundreds of pictures. The hard part was editing them to a managable quantity and attaching them to the writer's text. ❧ The writer, Mark Bernstein, is no stranger to New Bremen. His formidable historical retrospective of New Bremen from day one, the book, *New Bremen*, made him the only choice for observing the town from the perspective of a new century. He was welcomed back, and interviewed more than forty citizens for this text. ❧ Of course, the real kudos must go to the citizens of New Bremen, without whom the photographer, the writer, the underwiter (Crown Equipment Corporation), and the publisher would have had little to work with. From there, real excellence is in paying attention to the details. And those details included expert guidance from Crown's Marketing Communications Department, specifically, Bill Klosterman; logistics provided by Pam Bergman; Crown's Dee Fledderjohn, who shared her knowledge of names and faces; and Graphica with their expertise for cover design. We hope that Orange Frazer has made the collected efforts of all of these people — along with Jim Dicke II, whose intrinsic understanding of the need to document history for those who come after — into a work that keeps the pleasure of holding a book at its highest form.

— *Marcy Hawley*
*Publisher*

*Table of Contents*

New Bremen 2000

*L*ate in the evening of December 31, 1999, the town of New Bremen, Ohio, joined the world in moving into a new century.  Much is arbitrary in life, but it is not arbitrary to ask just what New Bremen carried on its journey into the new age.

*Passage*

This essay takes a stroll through New Bremen. It follows Monroe Street, but digresses to include the Serendipity preschool at St. Paul United Church of Christ and the roadwork undertaken in late 1999 on Main. The stroll touches on Walt Schmitmeyer's barbershop, Ginny Winner's hairstyling shop, the New Bremen Rod & Gun Club, and the new high school.

It attempts to answer, at least implicitly, certain questions about New Bremen: who comes to town; who speaks for the town; who listens to it, teaches it, and protects it. This writing is based primarily on interviews conducted with forty-five New Bremen residents in the final two months of the century. Not all those interviewed will find their names here, but all their comments became part of the mix from which the essay was drawn.

Some while back, New Bremen mayor Robert Klein approached local writer/artist Daniel Keyes with the suggestion that Keyes give a serious look at the existing village seal and consider possibilities for its improvement. The village seal, Keyes noted, was only a variation of the State of Ohio seal, and he urged the village to create a new one.

In his research, Keyes did not find any particular strong association for New Bremen, for example, as Pittsburgh was so strongly associated with steel. He did, however, pin down three generalities. First, that New Bremen has been a place of opportunity. Second, that it has been a peaceful place. Third, that is has been a prosperous place. "Not rich," he noted, "but people did well."

With that, Keyes tentatively designated PROMISE, PEACE, PROSPERITY as the seal's motto. For the design, he wanted a canal boat — New Bremen's location on the Miami-Erie Canal led to its first prosperity. He wanted an element from the Ohio seal, and chose the sun. The seal's central image is of a boat sailing through opening canal doors. The boat sails forward, Keyes' design suggests, at the beckoning of a figure. God, if you wish; a pioneer, if you prefer. The sunshine represents peace; the beckoning figure represents promise; the opening floodgates represent prosperity. The 42-inch wide original can be seen at the village building on the wall between the dispatcher's office and that of Police Chief Doug Harrod.  So, if the central question is: What does New Bremen take of itself into the next century?  The answer begins with Promise, Peace, Prosperity.

A gush of water carries a canal boat into a welcoming future, as depicted on the town's official seal. In one sense, the seal is about gaining the opportunity to work. New Bremen has always had a conditional optimism: If what is required is work, then that requirement will be met.

*Top left:* Sold under names like J. M. Brucken, cigars were for years a minor New Bremen industry.

***Bottom left:*** That industry passed, as did New Bremen Speedway, the half-mile dirt track that offered more thrills than a small town is usually allowed to have. Today, its grandstand sits in immobile decay.

*Right:* Surviving both cigars and car racing was Harry Ludeka. As a young man, Ludeka was advised by a physician to avoid marriage — his constitution might not be up to it. In January 2000, Harry turned 102. Born in 1898, he has taken part in three centuries, just like New Bremen itself. Here, he holds a pre-World War One photo of himself.

*Left:* Nobody's done it longer. Hoffman Decorating is the longest continuously operating business in New Bremen. They are, as their business card states, 'Professionals in Painting & Papering Since 1875.'

*Top right:* Possibly as old, though past redecorating, is this dilapidated outhouse, collapsed a distance from Route 66A.

*Bottom right:* From near that outhouse, one can see a log wall, an intact remnant of post-Civil War days.

*Left:* Drew Meyer, president of the New Bremen Historical Society, and a chalkboard upon which local students learned the Palmer alphabet. This graceful lettering was favored in the days before typewriters, when everything was recorded by hand and everyone's lettering had to be readable.

*Right:* Statue of a farmer and his dog, carved from rough granite by Christ Grothaus at German Township farm on Route 274, east of New Bremen. Grothaus wished to be buried near this site. Before he finished carving his tombstone, however, Grothaus was fatally injured in the field by his pet bull.

$\mathcal{A}$ certain amount of grumbling occurred at

Bolly's Restaurant when the crew from E. J. Meyer

of Ottawa arrived in October to rip out the five

blocks of Main Street that run north from Monroe,

passing Bolly's on the way.

Exercising the prerogative of experience, Urban Seger, Dick Bergman, Leonard Liesner, Cletus Niekamp, Leo Schwartz and Linus Schulze take up vantage outside Bolly's to see what the day and the street have to offer. And make a counteroffer.

*Main Street*

The street was getting a complete overhaul.  The roadbed was stripped bare.  New water and sewer lines would be laid; new storm drains and gas lines installed.  New curbs and gutters.  Finally, dirt and gravel would be compacted on the roadbed and covered by nine inches of blacktop applied in three layers.

A street has a history.  Main Street once lay on the path of Route 66 and was the route the interurban cars took through town.  It was at the corner of Main and Monroe that in 1909 an interurban car jumped the tracks and two people were killed.  When times were tight during the Depression, the interurban tracks were ripped up and sold for scrap to Minster Forge.  A street is also a time capsule, preserving whatever was underneath its surface when the pavement was poured.  When workers stripped off the surface of Main Street, they discovered a sewer line near First and Main Streets had, for years, been plugged with a six-inch cannonball.

The work meant some inconvenience for those who lived along the street.  Residents parked their cars in alleys or on nearby side streets and made somewhat longer grocery-laden trots to their back doors.  In compensation, they will get a better roadway, and — with copper pipes replacing lead — better tasting water.  As an aesthetic improvement, the old, somewhat gangly two-story green street lamps will be replaced by low, stylish black ones.

No one at Bolly's was opposed to any of this.  What motivated the grumbling was concern that the work would interfere with the card game that takes place every day at 1 p.m., generally after the players have lunched on Bolly's special.

Bolly's, said co-owner Bryan Trego, is the last of New Bremen's great hangouts.  Wints' drew the younger crowd and Hotel Hollingsworth catered more to those of drinking age, but both shut down years ago.  Bolly's remains.  Its counter carries a softball trophy; a 'Lil Drug Store' display that dispenses Tylenol and a chalked announcement of the day's special: Mushroom steak, mashed potatoes and gravy; green beans.  The prices are reasonable — $1.50 for blueberry pancakes — and the muffins are from scratch.

❧

Trego surveyed the street. For the past several weeks, work on the street has forced his regulars to park farther away. Still, he said, the work has moved right along. "All our regulars are pretty faithful." As he speaks, a faithful regular comes in.

'What can I get for you, Leonard?'

The customer, brightly: 'I'll have the dinner.'

At 1 p.m., the game begins, blue cards at a red table. Card playing in New Bremen is denominational. At the Senior Citizens Center, the game of choice is euchre. Bolly's is devoutly rummy. "You might lose 50 cents in an afternoon," said Jerry Brown, who is then daunted to discover he is already down that amount at only 2:15 p.m.

Shuffle and deal. Five minutes to play a hand with conversation throughout. "Now, Delphos St. John," said one player, referring to a standing power in small high school football, "when they first came into the league, they were so bad they almost gave up football. Then that new coach came in."

The card players are undistracted by the street work. The teeth of a brightly painted yellow, white and blue PC220LC Kamatsu shovel swung back and forth a few feet outside Bolly's front window. Nobody raised a head. Or missed a discard.

❧

In early November, the pounding outdoors on Main Street reverberated the office floor of New Bremen postmaster Dale Monnier. By report, the postmaster said, "they're going to be done by Christmas." Monnier has served successively as postmaster of Fort Recovery, Arcanum and New Bremen. All small towns. "These are places that are kept up really well. They're about the same in community pride. In some towns, they don't have the money to do the streets."

New Bremen does. The village would pay for the Main Street improvements with money from a .5 percent local income tax enacted in 1993, and used since to finance such improvements as the new water tower and the new swimming pool.

Whatever residents may think, New Bremen's municipal income tax — the full rate is 1.5 percent — is highly popular with those who administer the village. The major share of the revenues produced by local income taxes goes to the city in which the taxpayer works, not the city in which he or she resides. This favors places which, like New Bremen, have many more people commuting in to work than leaving town to work elsewhere. The paychecks of those who commute to New Bremen, former mayor Urban Buschur observed, "are in town just long enough for us to tax them." Long enough, that is, to help pay for five new blocks on Main Street.

New Bremen closed the twentieth century as a prospering place. By the 1990 census, its average household income of $38,704 was 13 percent above the state average. Given the recent strength of the local economy, the year 2000 census will likely show a larger differential. A measure of New Bremen's prosperity is its number of industrial jobs. The 1999 Harris Ohio Industrial Directory gives that number as 3,283 — more than the population of the village itself. The largest share, of course, is at the Crown Equipment Corporation, but even without Crown, New Bremen has a substantial and growing industrial base.

Greg Myers, executive director of the Southwestern Auglaize County Chamber of Commerce, said, "To have this number of skilled jobs goes hand in hand with the German sense of prosperity. People have to make a good living to maintain things at a particular standard, to maintain their homes. For generations, it's been a good solid economy here."

Some combination of wealth, judgment and coordination — public, private and volunteer — has brought New Bremen accoutrements of the good life. Village manager Anthony Bales ticked off a list: the new high school, the new swimming pool, a well-maintained infrastructure, the Bremenfest Park, the renovated downtown, the new library.

Bales has been village manager since mid-1998. He sought a village post, rather than a state or federal one, he said, because he likes the close association between small town government and those it serves. "When people have a problem," he said, "they know who to call." For example, Lois Moeller, confronted with a wasps' nest outside her door, called the police. Chief Doug Harrod came by, determined that the nest was dormant and, with a long stick lent by Moeller, dispatched it.

As village manager, Bales directs the village's street, water, sewer and electrical departments. As 1999 closed, New Bremen was suing Dayton Power & Light over how much DP&L charges for the current it delivers in bulk. Sturdily independent, New Bremen owned the electrical poles, lines, grid and substation since 1908, when locally owned electrical powered was initiated. Sturdily independent, and frugal. The basic electric rate in New Bremen is 5.5 cents a kWh, well below a regional average of 8.9 cents.

Small town politics is intimate. During the 1999 election, Bales realized that voters were not simply electing a mayor, they were also electing Bales' boss. The boss elected — actually re-elected — was Robert Klein, who gained his second term as mayor by a 409-334 margin over Paul Maurer.

The mayor is the chief executive officer of the village. Klein grew up locally, more on a farm than in town, and worked at Stamco, Crown and now for Minster Machine. Being mayor is about a one-third time job, paying $5,500. As mayor, Klein chairs meetings of village council and votes in the event of a tie. Twice a month he holds mayor's court, where infractions of local ordinances are heard. He performs the occasional marriage, does "a lot of PR" on behalf of the village, and hears the complaints.

Likely, there will be more. The state highway department, Klein said, has budgeted funds to resurface Route 66 from Schwieterman's pharmacy at the Monroe Street stoplight to the Wendy's at the south end of town. Past resurfacings have left little curb remaining. Council, Klein says, is considering re-doing the curbs and sidewalks simultaneous to the resurfacing and possibly redoing the infrastructure.

There will be advantages, the mayor said. Traffic lights on Washington Street will be controlled by sensors. They will remain green, unless a car on a cross street triggers a stop. That, he said, will improve traffic flow. There is a downside. For the period running from late June until early November 2000, someone will have to figure out where to put the 8,000 cars that now use Washington Street each day.

*Left:* Spreading the news. Postmaster Jenny Fox oversees an operation that moves nearly 10,000 letters to and from townspeople each day. Mail delivery is now more formalized: until the 1920s, New Bremen residences had no street numbers; everybody simply knew where everybody lived. *Right:* Spreading the light. Workmen set the braces that will support North Main Street's new street lamps.

The rebuilding of North Main Street was the village's last improvement of the 1990s. Sewer, storm, water and gas lines were installed; the old street surface was rebuilt with dirt, stone and three layers of blacktop. *Left:* Workmen in trench check the new lines for level. *Right:* A barricade screens pedestrians away from the work site.

Top: Dean Waterman with the newspaper, Don Stienecker of New Knoxville and Alan Bushman get caught up with news and each other at Bolly's.
Bottom: No sharp edges. Hands roughened by work and weather. Cards softened by hands and time.

Card sharks. Don't let the smiles fool you. This is one slick group of card players, which gathers daily at Bolly's for an after lunch game of gin rummy. [back row] Dick Bergman, David Paul, Cletus Niekamp [front row], Paul Niekamp, Leonard Liesner and Leo Schwartz.

The grumbling about Main Street worked its way up the block and around the corner where it made lodgment in the barber chairs of Walt Schmitmeyer, and diversified. Some days it took the form of commiseration with the continuing travails of Pete Rose, ballplayer. Other times it was about the wonder of a rising Dow, and musing about how long that rise would continue.

*Barber Pole*

Walt Schmitmeyer attended barber college in Columbus, where he learned the Andrew technique for cutting hair, which he has done in New Bremen since 1958.  Today, Walt cuts hair in a 12- by 16-foot shop with a floor of red linoleum and a scattering of Coca-Cola memorabilia and six shelves of hair care products.

A customer asked, "Are all your clippers Y2K compliant?"

They aren't, but Schmitmeyer is.  He has brought out sets of manual clippers, unused since the 1940s, just in case the century ends in one mass  power outage.  "Not much rain — that's also Y2K," he said, predicting "no rain or cold thereafter."

In the 1960s, the Beatles and the wish of young men to adopt their shaggy style wreaked havoc with the barbering world.  Three of every ten barbers hung up their clippers. Schmitmeyer went to seminars in Toledo and Cleveland to learn the new styles.  Short styles returned, but not the barbers to clip them.  The average barber today, Walt says, is 66.  Which makes him glad to have an assistant, a young New Bremen man named Glenn Schieb, whose mother presented him to Walt some years ago with the words, "He likes to cut hair."

Having an assistant gives Schmitmeyer a luxury few area barbers enjoy; he can take time off.

People in barber chairs, with nowhere to go and nothing much to do, talk.  About the travails of Pete Rose.  About the wonders of a rising Dow.  Schmitmeyer, often, talks back. "They say stay away from politics and religion, but I don't," he said.  "I'm an old German and I just like to let it go. Sometimes I stir it up a little bit.  Naturally, I try to get them to agree with me.  Some diehard Clinton fans came in — that was probably the last good argument."

Conversation continued.  A customer said, "I just got hold of an interesting fact. Two women got killed by lightning in England.  Coroner said they were killed because they were wearing underwire bras."

Walt responded, "That'll happen."

*Left:* In his West First Street shop, long-time village barber Ernie Phlipot leans over the chair that has supported half the heads of hair of New Bremen.
*Top right:* Judging by Phlipot's sign, barber's hours beat banker's hours.
*Bottom right:* Phlipot's current location is a bit quieter than his previous one, which featured slot car races to which his customers brought their entries.

"*People* worry about being too clean.  When I was working construction, every sandwich I picked up had fingerprints on it." — *Paul Westerbeck, Carpenter*

Some years back, Goodyear went on strike, leaving James Hudson with time on his hands. His wife, Anna Mae, persuaded him to share her avid interest in auctions. He went, picked up furniture that needed work, and brought it home. The renovated furniture accumulated. Anna Mae opened her Anns'tiques, she says, somewhat in self-defense — so furniture would flow out as well as in. She maintains a particular fondness for furniture made in New Bremen by, successively, the Heinfeld, Klanke and Auglaize furniture companies.

*Top left:* Jenny Ronnebaum readies the coffee at Bolly's.
*Top right:* Mary Ellen Minnich outside the former Minnich's Carryout, whose candy, pop and other treats drew children from the nearby swimming pool.
*Bottom left:* Tire in hand, Crown employee Jim Eyink works to return to service a company-owned vehicle at Crown's service center on South Washington Street.
*Bottom right:* Bob Monsell pauses on his route, delivering the *Penny Saver* by bicycle.

The adult life of Dave Kuck, Sr. has focused on fire. At his welding shop, fire is his tool. As New Bremen's long-time fire chief, fire was his foe. But friend or foe, it merits a healthy regard.

*Top:* Jack Thobe, left, and Jim Brining of Kinninger Production Welding confer next to stacks of overhead guards welded in their shop. In recent years, Kinninger's joined other companies that gained expanded quarters by moving to the Bunker Hill Industrial Park on Route 274.

*Bottom:* At Crown Plant 1, Maggie Silverthorn of Sidney and Linda Grillot of New Bremen work with 'wound bobbins' that conduct electricity to the antenna drives of TV rotators, one of the company's earliest products, still in demand.

*Left:* Annette Thompson, curator of New Bremen's prime tourist attraction, the Bicycle Museum of America, stands by a 1950 Huffy Convertible. The museum has more than 200 bikes on display, beginning with a German-made 1816 Draissine.

*Top right:* Edith Wissman taught music in the local schools, gave piano lessons in her home and for 19 years directed the St. Paul church choir. People, she believes, should hear Bach and Beethoven to learn to listen; most will like best the music popular when they were young adults. "My husband and I like Big Band. My mother likes to listen to gospel."

*Left:* Dave and Gene Roediger ready their new rotary harrow, one of the first put in service in Auglaize County. The new harrow, Gene says, "fluffs the stalks up," so that the fields dry more rapidly, allowing earlier planting — including planting of soybeans, which is what they plan for this field.

*Top right:* German Township farm fields are rich, but often low-lying. To draw off that water, fields are underlain with drainage tile, like that produced by the New Bremen Underground Pipe Company. Company employee Luke Walker checks recent output at the company's Route 66A production site.

*Bottom right:* Cutters used to slot and shape steel at the Auglaize Erie Machine Incorporated. Back to the tinsmiths of a century-and-a-half ago, New Bremen has had expertise at turning metal to task.

*Left:* Workman at the spire of the empty Zion Reformed church building. The congregation, established in 1865 when nine families withdrew from the St. Peter United Church of Christ, held largely English-language services from the first. In 1975, the Zion congregation dissolved; many of its former members then joined Faith Alliance Church, now located near Route 66.

*Top right:* Myra Holzer and Donna Cormier, farm manager, turning out the horses at Jo-Mi Arabians farm on Route 66A, where Holzer has worked with Arabians since 1979.

*Bottom right:* The workshop of carpenter Paul Westerbeck, with the remnants of past projects and the essentials of current ones.

For Sale
RE/MAX MLS
Lowell Ziegenbusch
RE/MAX
One
629-

"My father was superintendent of bridges for the state highway department," New Bremen dentist Ron Riebel said. "He farmed 88 acres. We'd go into Asheville — drive in to get the newspapers — and all the old guys would call out, 'Hey, Grover' and 'Howdy, Grove,' and for some reason that stuck with me. I thought I'd like to have a town like that some day."



Real estate agent Lowell Ziegenbusch puts a home on the market in New Bremen's Pioneer Subdivision. With good times, New Bremen's population rose twenty percent in the 1990s; Pioneer housed many of the new faces.

A town, that is, where people hail you by name. As it happened, Riebel wasn't hailed in New Bremen, he was recruited. At a New Bremen High School reunion, Mayor Frank Dicke compared notes with a visiting Lowell McNett and learned that McNett's wife worked at the dental school of Ohio State University. New Bremen had had no dentist for twelve years, and Frances McNett agreed to help locate one. Riebel was invited to town, where he approvingly noted that "the homes were well cared for, the leaves were up" and decided on New Bremen. "Been here 31 years," he said today. "Love the small size; love bumping into patients at the store."

There have been two immigrations to New Bremen. The first, in the 1830s and 1840s, populated the town with newcomers from the German States. They came to Oheio — as they first spelled it — to find unhampered space in which they could maintain their customs, speak their language and raise their children and their crops. For decades thereafter, New Bremen was dominated by the descendents of these original families.

New Bremen is today receiving its second wave of immigration — a steady arrival of newcomers who have no strong existing ties to the village. Perhaps one-fourth of those who move to New Bremen come to work for the Crown Equipment Corporation, the town's largest employer. Some move for convenience: a couple settled in town because one worked in Sidney and the other in Greenville and New Bremen was in between. Others are young people who grew up in town, went to college, lived for a time in a city and are now moving back to New Bremen to raise a family.

But whether the property is an older home on Franklin Street or newly built in the Pioneer subdivision, chances are it sells for more than if it was located in St. Marys, Celina or Wapakoneta. Realtor Lowell Ziegenbusch puts the premium people pay to buy into New Bremen at $10,000. What they gain for that premium, he added, is "quality of life." What realtor Barbara Ziegenbusch called, "Pride of ownership. Well-maintained properties. Strong work ethic." What realtor Marilyn Schwartz described as, "Something safer. The crime rate is low; school system is excellent."

Today, when someone says they are building a home, it means they have hired a contractor. In the 1830s, it meant they were felling and debarking trees. Still, there is some commonality between what draws newcomers today and what drew the first settlers to New Bremen.  In a changing world, the village offers a place to make a reasonable life.

**Left:** Herman Street in New Bremen, quiet to begin with, is muffled almost into silence by a thick layering of snow.
**Right:** Taking advantage of conditions, a snow bunny, Ella Kraimer, is an easy rider.

*Top:* A porch on Main Street, and a powerful Midwestern image, here fleshed out in New Bremen by the Kraimer family of South Main: Jim, Whitney and children.
*Bottom:* Front porches, back yards, the two natural habitats of the family. Here, the Jeff and Holly Bertke family enjoys time outside.

*Top:* As any child knows, sidewalks are not pathways for grownups, but long skinny playgrounds. As the natural province of the young, they exist for hopscotch, jump rope and spontaneous works of art.
*Bottom:* New Bremen gathers at the table. Here, the table of Jim and Whitney Kraimer welcomes relatives from Chicago. Meals are about more than food. New Bremen school officials, asked to what they attribute success of local students, invariably cite the meal time families spend together.

*Left:* These streets were made for skating. New Bremen teens, wind behind them, glide along Water Street, ready to repel invasion, or join one.

*Right:* Collectors' kitchen. Viola Headapohl takes to the window and Allie makes a first-ever jump for the chair in a kitchen that shows its owners' interests. Paul Headapohl collects: mobiles, things with handles — pitchers, mugs and such — and more. The bugs on the cupboard, a gift from a grandson, turned up later in one of Paul's prized floral arrangements. His decorations are the visual grace note to historical museum dinners, weddings, library functions, mother-daughter dinners and other events at St. Paul Church.

$\mathcal{T}$hose moving to New Bremen are changed by and, in turn, change the town. Not least, those moving to New Bremen have made it larger. By census count, New Bremen had 2,563 residents in 1990. By estimate of the Ohio Department of Development, it reached 3,075 in 1998.



The view from the bell tower of the St. Paul United Church of Christ. New Bremen built itself of brick and wood, the first invariably red, the latter most often painted white. Built of natural materials, the town shows its age well.

If accurate, that is an eight-year increase of twenty percent, the most rapid of any city, town or township in Auglaize County. One New Bremen resident frames the town's expansion by saying, "When I was a kid, if you could ride your bike to Lock Two it meant you were getting big. Now, I can just about see Lock Two from my street."

New Bremen is changed, too, by changes in the broader culture. Historically, New Bremen was not only small, but insular. Within the German-dominated reaches of Auglaize County, families rarely moved from one town to another. Thus, not only were names German, but a given German name was often associated with a particular town. Dr. James Luedeke observed, "At one time, everybody knew by last name what town someone was from. Luedeke was mostly New Bremen; some Celina. Wierwille, Paul, Sunderman, Knost, Kuenning, Kellermeyer, Boesel — those meant New Bremen."

The great virtues that settled the Midwest were work, religion, cleanliness, sobriety and thrift. New Bremen, being German, cut back some on sobriety and doubled up on cleanliness and thrift. One long-time resident stated, "I remember my mother saying it was the only place she knew where people swept the streets." There is, said the Rev. Lawrence Holmer, "a sort of a standing joke about who gets the mower out first in the spring. As soon as someone mows, then my grass starts to look a little long." Stories of financial frugality abound. "It used to be," one resident said, "that you postponed repair on a house until after the assessment was complete." That way, the extra tax the improvement brought was not payable until the following reassessment.

As a precept, cleanliness is still observed. Thrift, however, has suffered broad attack. In barely a generation, a country built on thrift is gorging itself on easy credit. "The biggest change from my youth," said Dave Pape, an accountant in New Bremen since 1951, "is the credit people are allowed. In my youth, you had to have cash — for a car or for something for the house. With credit, you don't have to save." Dr. James Luedeke noted, "The older generation came over with very little. They were used to getting little at Christmas and birthdays. Today, people go into debt to have things sooner." Thrift was more than a financial strategy, it was a moral precept. Pay as you go meant, among other things, don't get ahead of yourself. Don't take anything for granted. The change may be more apparent than real. Dave Pape observed, "Some can save; some can't. In high school, I had a teacher who told me that if you divided all the money up equally then the same people would end up with it."

New Bremen was founded as "a town for Germans of Protestant faith." Today, it is culturally more German than anything else. It is, that is to say, a German town with a Chinese takeout. It is German, musically. Edith Wissman noted, "At church, we tend to sing the old German songs more enthusiastically than the new ones." It is German in its discipline and its limits. One high school teacher said, "You can get the students to do anything you want up to a certain point, because the German heritage will accept the discipline. The downside is that the kids only go so far. They're not inclined to challenge; to push themselves." One New Bremen resident of German descent describes his  heritage in words non-Germans might not consider compliments: 'Stubborn. Tight-fisted, perhaps. But good workers.' What remains, and what most  characterizes the town, is the cultural injunction that one be usefully engaged in something.  One must work.

James F. Dicke II said, "With New Bremen, you start with a German heritage.  They are pretty particular people. Sometimes stubborn.  A great sense of humor.  They party, but are serious about their work.  The highest compliment you can pay someone here is: 'Oh, him, I know him, he's a good worker.'  The making of this community is that it is made by pretty good people."

In a sense, changes brought by growing size and changing culture are generic. They could affect any place small and distinctive.  New Bremen has also been changed by something local, by the growth since the Second World War of the Crown Equipment Corporation, of which James F. Dicke II is president.

"An uncle of mine," Dicke said, "thought I should consider becoming a medical doctor.  That didn't appeal to me except as it was my uncle who suggested it.  I think medicine offers less of a sense of creativity.  If you're a surgeon, you fix something that's broken.  In the end, everybody dies; you're engaged in a holding action.  I always thought being involved in the family business, or any type of business, was an opportunity to build. There's a creative satisfaction from building a business."

Crown has had three readily identifiable influences on New Bremen. First, it is by a wide measure the largest employer in town. Second, it took the lead in reconstructing the village's downtown. And third, through its Pioneer subdivision, it created the largest housing development in New Bremen.

"We've been accused of having some master plan," Dicke said, "Actually, there was none." Downtown, Crown purchased and renovated declining buildings, which were then used by Crown as office space or leased to others. This represented a dovetailing of needs. First, Crown's own growth brought with it the need for added office space. Second, Crown was marketing itself by bringing customers to town to show the company at work. Showcasing itself showcased downtown, which by the late 1970s was losing its vitality. The two concerns combined to prompt Crown's efforts.

Crown's engagement in Pioneer, Dicke said, was in part by default. "To an extent," he said, "Crown moved on Pioneer because the town itself was not large enough to attract a commercial developer." The development, one resident said, "was a great factor in opening up New Bremen. To be able to bring to town the skills you need, you have to provide the housing. If not, the people you want won't come."

There is peripheral concern in New Bremen that Crown may be too central an influence. One minister said, "Crown has been so involved with the community in positive ways, in ways that enhance. There is a fear of what would happen if Crown goes public and the community finds itself involved with a public corporation rather than a family one."

James Dicke II downplays that concern. "The potential exists," he said, "that Crown could be too dominant. But look at New Bremen over the past 100 years. There's a constant need for a place to remake itself. At one time, it was the woolen mills that were the major employer. Then, White Mountain [dairy]. Then, Stamco. It used to be said that you worked at Crown because you couldn't get a job at Stamco." He added, "For the foreseeable future, we've no plans to move our headquarters from New Bremen or to go public."

To balance Crown's strength, the New Bremen Community

Improvement Corporation was formed to help diversify the local economy. CIC has pursued a double strategy: first, hold existing industry in town by providing better locations in the CIC-created Bunker Hill Industrial Park; second, use that park to draw in new industry. Success, thus far, has been more with the former than the latter.

When James Brining and Jack Thobe purchased Kinninger Production Welding, a local company, in 1994, a new site was a priority. The company then operated from quarters near Main Street. Among other problems, there was no loading dock and everything had to be loaded and unloaded by hand. They considered moving out of town, Thobe said, then decided on 16,000 square feet of rented space in Bunker Hill. Under new management, Kinninger has grown from seven employees to nineteen.

The New Bremen Machine & Tool Co. moved to Bunker Hill in 1997 from a site near the new swimming pool. The firm is firmly local, dating to 1928. Its vice presidents, Randy and Jay Bergman, signed on in the seventh grade, when they started sweeping the floor for their father, still a co-owner. The company builds unique tool and die sets that allow its customers — Harley, GM, Volvo trucks, Navistar, Honda and others — to turn out finished parts by the tens of thousands. One such set weighed 19 tons and is worth $168,000. The challenge, Randy Bergman said, "is being able to make things. We're known for being able to do complicated parts." The firm had six employees in 1992; now, it employs forty.

Two views of New Bremen, both from across the former Miami-Erie Canal. The canal connected New Bremen to the world, but was an uncertain asset — each year, winter closed it to traffic. ***Bottom:*** From the canal, New Bremen scales gently up to Main and Franklin Streets.

*Left*: New Bremen's twin peaks — of St. Peter and St. Paul church, respectively. In their pews, much of the town for generations found its communion with itself, its neighbors and its God.

*Top right*: New Bremen's signature block, wonderfully restored. Right half, completed in 1897, was the village's new center: fire station, mayor's office, town council chamber and, when events warranted, jail.

*Bottom right*: New Bremen's best view is afforded by the "penthouse" built above the Schwieterman pharmacy. Here, from that site, is the look to the northwest.

*Left:* Door of an empty building on North Main Street. Given the town's talent for salvaging its past, that door may yet open to some new incarnation.

*Top right:* The Mideast had its fertile crescent, Auglaize County, its golden triangle — New Knoxville, Minster and New Bremen — which together claim most of the county's industrial wealth. Through the glass, Gregory Myers, who as executive director of the 'triangle's' Chamber of Commerce, spreads the good word.

*Bottom right:* Corner of Monroe and Main, where the interurban once jumped the track. The town clock still keeps current time.

*Left:* In a town full of notable restorations, perhaps the most remarkable of all is this Queen Anne house, relocated to the Crown farm and painstakingly restored to its former splendor.

*Top right:* The old mill at Lock Two. The canal made New Bremen and its environs a center of industry — grain was milled, hogs were slaughtered, travelers arrived and were suitably impressed by the bustle of the place.

*Bottom right:* New Bremen rewards an eye for detail, like that of this facade design on East First Street.

A four-year old demonstrates the casual tact of the young.  Pointing to a girl in a  pink dress, she says, "This is my best friend."  Then, pointing to a girl in a blue sweater, added,  "This is my other best friend." And finally to a girl in a red jumper, "And my other best friend."  No one else being within earshot, that's all the best friends she claimed for the moment.

Serendipitans

The setting is a classroom-sized space in New Bremen's St. Paul's Church, where Ann Kuhn and her four assistants operate Serendipity School for three-, four- and five-year olds. The children swarm about. One in a Cleveland football T-shirt reports that the Browns won the previous weekend. "My dad missed the end but my mom saw it." Another asks, "Do you know what my job is? I'm Ryne — I'm the flag holder." The church is a tolerant landlord. "Noise is our byproduct," Kuhn acknowledged. "No one minds."

Kuhn is asked about her charges. "Being four in New Bremen? The typical child in town lives a very wonderful life. Most don't want for anything material. But it's not just material. They are happy because they come from happy homes with parents who care for them, parents who say, 'What do I need to do?'"

At Serendipity, much of what the children do is hands-on — Pla-Doh and puzzles and a table whose top lifts off to reveal an indoor sandbox. "A lot of people differ with hands on," Kuhn said, "They use mimeograph sheets. 'Today, I'm going to show you how to make an "A".'" That is not Kuhn's way. "What you hear comes and goes," she said. "What you do stays with you."

Snack time, red juice and Ritz crackers. A short prayer, composed by one of the students: "Dear God. Thank you for Indians and turkeys and food for turkeys and pumpkins. Amen." Settling the children for story time, Kuhn says, "If I open my eyes, do we all have listening ears?" Mostly, they do. Before reading '*Twas the Night Before Thanksgiving*,' Kuhn asked what they know of the holiday.

"The Pilgrims invited the Indians, why?"

"Because they brought all the food."

Later, the children will pay the school's thirtieth annual visit to a turkey farm near New Knoxville. Certain events are traditional. An annual Easter Buckeye Hunt is held in a woods near town that Kuhn salts with buckeyes the evening before. Staff members and animals from Bruckner's Nature Center visit. Afterwards, the children vote a favorite. The snake always wins.

Kuhn is in her 36th year of directing the school. "I feel blessed that I found a niche. People say: 'What about retirement?' I have ten signed on for the incoming list for 2003."

Top: What you are told fades, Anne Kuhn believes. What you do stays with you. Here, the Serendipity School director is hands-on with Chrissy Adams [left] and Jill McClurg.

Below: Painter Henri Matisse was asked why his work became more colorful and flowing as he aged. Because, the painter replied, it takes a long time to see like a child. Unless you are one. Artwork here courtesy of Madison Barlage, Serendipity School.

$\mathcal{D}$escribing the inner life of New Bremen, the Reverend Lawrence Holmer, retired pastor of St. Peter's United Church of Christ, said, "The given within the culture is to 'keep it to oneself.'  Often, very little is expressed.  In my own family — Germans — little would be said to the children, or not discussed, or, if discussed, discussed in German."



The spire of the St. Peter United Church of Christ transects the horizon in this view from the bell tower of neighboring St. Paul. Before the rise of industry, church steeples claimed the horizons of American cities and towns, providing both spiritual reminder and geographic orientation. In New Bremen, where little is more than two stories high, the church spires still stand out.

Similar thoughts are offered up by others whose work admits them to the town's private heart. Fr. Dan Conlon of Holy Redeemer Catholic Church said, "People like to maintain a certain exterior calm. It's not very accepted to let your anxieties show. There's a sense of responsibility to observe the common sense of well-being; not to interfere." The Rev. John Tostrick, associate pastor at St. Paul's United Church of Christ, commented, "People here are not histrionic; it's part of the German heritage."

The quiet, Father Conlon suggested, reflects the fact that "people believe they will be helped by family and close friends. There are large extended families here upon which people rely." Similarly, the Rev. Tostrick noted, "Families tend to be private. So when they say something, you know it's important."

When they speak, what do they say?

New Bremen, said Father Conlon, "is almost ideal. Good jobs. It's small. Virtually no crime. Prospering. Virtually no poverty. Still, you expect a degree of anxiety in people's personal situations. Even the most ideal town can't prevent divorce. Teens and drugs. Adolescent rebellion. The town can't guarantee everyone's happiness and a good harvest every year."

Individually, the concerns expressed are those that one might imagine. How to be a good person, a good parent, a good spouse. How to seek redress for grievance, or contrition for having aggrieved. How to accept loss, or good fortune.

Far more likely today, that conversation occurs in a confessional. The town was established by and for Protestants. For years, anyone in Auglaize County asked what distinguished Minster and New Bremen would likely answer that the former was Catholic and the latter Protestant. When retired pharmacist Dave Schwieterman was a child in New Bremen in the 1930s, his was one of only seven Catholic families in town. Today, Catholicism is the faith of half or more of the town; Holy Redeemer is easily New Bremen's largest congregation. There's no particular agreement as to how this shift occurred. Some suggest that when Protestant-owned farms in German Township came to market in the 1930s, many were purchased by Catholic families. Others speculate that it happened as local industries expanded and reached farther for employees.

Whatever their denomination, people in New Bremen in

their religious life affirm themselves not by challenging tradition, but by embracing it. When, for example, a wedding ceremony is planned, one local clergyman noted, "It is not common for people to want to bring in things that are extraneous from a liturgical point of view. They don't set out to make their wedding as different as possible." They are not laying claim to marriage, marriage is laying claim to them. Regard for convention extends to the wedding supper. In a city, reception guests might stand while eating ham sandwiches or sit while being served filet mignon. In New Bremen, the menu is more predictable: "Beef in gravy or juice; fried chicken; two kinds of stuffing — one with raisins — noodles; corn, cole slaw, roll and cake for dessert. This is not a criticism, but a statement that the event is central to the individuals, not the reverse."

If New Bremen has a collective focus for its concern, that focus would be its young. There is, says Father Conlon, "great concern about young people. The schools reflect that concern. There is a real genuine concern about education." With the young, a second clergyman stated, "There is concern about drugs. There should be more concern with alcohol. It's accepted, because beer is a part of the German tradition."

Clergymen — and others in town — express the wish for a place where young people could congregate, as once they did at Wints', or the soda fountain at Schwieterman's pharmacy, or the ice cream shop on Monroe Street. The Rev. Tostrick would like to see "a wholesome place where kids can go out; be safe and unthreatened. Fifth- and sixth-graders on up. Where kids could go after school. Get a milkshake or a hamburger."

The clergy, of course, have concerns for the town.

"Sometimes," mused Lawrence Holmer, former minister of St. Peter's United Church of Christ, "the minister is the last to know." The Rev. Holmer sits in his Franklin Street living room, wearing a maroon sweatsuit and a considered expression. What is concerning Rev. Holmer is the decline in community he sees as following from New Bremen's growth and from change, generally. More and more, he says, there's an automatic aspect to life. "People move from the house to the car, from the car to the house. Paths don't cross that way. One of the most enjoyable things I recall, actually, was the Blizzard of '78. You couldn't drive; you were out in the street with each other. It was a common experience, with people relating to their neighbors in terms of relating to the storm."

New Bremen is not a place that frets. There is, one clergyman said, no communal hand wringing at all. There are, however, expectations. As Father Conlon stated, "I think what they look for here is that everybody pitches in and helps."

Prior to the Second World War, New Bremen was not only almost entirely German, but almost entirely Protestant as well. As were its churches.

*Left:* The main door of St. Paul's, New Bremen's oldest congregation.

*Right:* The tower of the former Zion Reformed Church.

NEW BREMEN
POLICE

At its core, New Bremen is a law-abiding place. Chief of Police Doug Harrod (directing traffic on South Washington) and his department work to keep that core from fraying.

$\mathscr{B}$y general consent, the largest collective disaster visited upon New Bremen in local memory was the Blizzard of '78, which sent temperatures to twenty below and drifted enough snow across Route 66 to close the highway.  Traffic ceased, and few wandered far.

The storm was a shared calamity.  Individual calamities, of course, occur.  A relative dies.  A couple divorces.  Rarely, though, is personal calamity in New Bremen the outcome of crime.  The village's crime rate is very low; no murder has been committed in town for 120 years.  There are at least two explanations for this circumstance, not mutually exclusive.

Doug Harrod, New Bremen Chief of Police since 1980, believes that New Bremen's relatively civil ways are sustained by the hands-on police work done by his six full-time and four part-time officers.  What deters crime, he said, is having the police out and about.  "My philosophy of crime prevention is to be visible," he said.  "If people see you, particularly at night, they don't cause trouble.  We have two cars on the road every night and we cover the entire village. We put a total of 100,000 miles on those cars each year."  New Bremen's police force, he said, is one of the few departments "where a policeman on patrol gets out of his vehicle to hand check the locks."

The  second  explanation  is  exemplified  by  an  1880s headline in *The New Bremen Sun.*  The newspaper was reporting on a break-in at a German Township farmhouse, which netted its perpetrators something less than $40 in goods.  In the largest size type the newspaper had, the headline described the act as the worst crime there was, "save only murder."  There was, within the culture, a simple horror of crime.  The line between right and wrong was forbiddingly clear to those émigré Germans who settled the town and who passed on their ways and values.  Law and culture ganged up on the would-be criminal.  To steal was not only illegal, it went against the precept that you must have nothing you had not earned.

In crisis, people cope.  During the Blizzard of '78, then-officer Jon Belton was dropped off at police headquarters bearing crockpots and necessities.  Townspeople running short on food or medicine called in to the station.  Howell's IGA supplied the food, payment deferred, with deliveries made by volunteers on snowmobile.  One man living on the edge of town called with what he presented as an urgent request: "I can't make it into town," he said, "but I got to have my chewing tobacco.  Can you send some out?"

Belton said: "We drew the line at that."

Chief Harrod
makes contact with
his officers.

The first Thursday evening Ginny Winner worked at Hair Performers she walked out the front door, "and about hit the deck." Gunfire. Rivers of it. The source of the sound proved no more menacing than the regular Thursday night shoot at the New Bremen Rod & Gun Club, several hundred yards up Route 274.

Gone Hunting

The Rod & Gun Club may be New Bremen's largest social club. Of its 216 current members, 118 are from the village. The club is organized for trapshooting, rifle shooting, black powder and archery. Its concrete block clubhouse measures about 70 x 28 and provides mounting room for a stuffed pheasant, a coyote, a trapped mink and eight deer heads. The four deer on the north wall are also functional — the electrical line to the speaker box is draped over their antlers.

In early November, several hundred gathered for the club's major fundraiser — its two-day Feather Party. Saturday evening is for serious talking and semi-serious poker. Eight tables, generally six at a table. Twenty dollars brings you forty red chips and entry into the first round. After two hours, those still in the game swap four red chips for one white one, and play on. They play until midnight, or until one player holds all the chips. By immediate recollection, $480 is the most anybody will claim or admit to winning.

Trapshooting has its satisfactions. "It's highly competitive," said Bill Woehrmyer. "I beat a top shooter in a Turkey Shoot and it made my day. My son, Dusty, there are some adult shooters who won't shoot against him. He was Northwest Ohio Zone Champion for subjuniors, under age 15." Most club members hunt. Rabbits, locally; deer in the counties above the Ohio River. Member John Belton said, "Eat the venison? Yes. Take the loin, slice and tenderize. It looks a bit like a minute steak, bread it and panfry it. Melts in your mouth."

By mid-afternoon Sunday, the clubhouse floor is littered with raffle tickets. Outside, one shooter stands with a cocked shotgun over his shoulder, ten more weapons lean against a gun rack, handmade of 2x6s and decking lumber. Contestants are playing a game called Murder. A clay pigeon is tossed. The first contestant shoots. If he misses, and the second shooter hits it, the first is eliminated from the match. If the second misses, but the third hits it, then one and two are both out. If the first shooter hits, and the second shoots anyway, the second is out. That's one round. Then, a new toss. The previous second shooter becomes the first shooter, and so on.

The club was formed November 13, 1956, holds a

99-year lease on its 27-acre property and plans to remain. Long-time club president Cy Niekamp said, "Rumors float around town that we're moving, but we're not for sale. Never will be for sale. As long as we keep our bullets on the property they can't do anything."

∽

A week after the Feather Party, twenty local Boy Scouts turned up for shooting and instruction, part of a state-mandated 15-hour course the Rod & Gun Club offers to meet the requirements for a state hunting license. With 44 members, New Bremen Boy Scout Troop #95 is the largest in the district. In November, its members took fundraising orders for popcorn, camped out near Stamco, had their shooting evening, delivered the popcorn and continued the task they share with the local Girl Scouts of recycling newspapers. None of which is as impressive as the time troop members concocted rabbit stew, Shepherd's pie and cheesecake cooking in Dutch ovens over a bed of charcoal.

Those who lead Boy Scouts and Girls Scouts do so on their own time. They are volunteers, and the voluntary urge is central to New Bremen.

In December, the Auglaize County Alumni Band — formerly the New Bremen Alumni Band — presented its Christmas Concert, collected $400 in donations and gave them to the choral program at the New Bremen High School, which did not charge for the use of its auditorium.

In December, the New Bremen Education Foundation — which raises and distributes about $25,000 a year in scholarship support to graduating seniors — began reviewing applications. All who apply receive something; in 1998-1999, awards ranging from $300 to $2000 were made to thirty local young people.

In December, the New Bremen Jaycees completed its annual Christmas tree sale, with the money going to Jaycee Park. The New Bremen Band Boosters is using the James F. Dicke Auditorium at the high school to draw better musical talent to town. Thus far, they have scheduled the Ohio Valley British Brass Band and the Northern University Show Choir and its Northernaires Jazz Quartet. In December, the local

American Legion Post #241, and its auxiliary, were organizing the New Year's Eve event it hosts for the town.  There are a number of other organizations, including the Friends of the Library, which raises money for children's craft programs and storytimes, and the New Bremen Historical Society, which maintains a museum on Main Street and publishes a newsletter.

Beyond these, there are the Lions Club, the New Bremen Senior Citizens, the Ohio Child Conservation League, the New Bremen Athletic Boosters, the New Bremen-New Knoxville Rotary Club, the Sons of the American Legion, the Woodmen of the World, the Cardinal Pride Association and many others not mentioned.  And the many organizers of Bremenfest — a three-day late summer event of music, food, socializing and games — that raises upwards of $100,000 for some community improvement, including Bremenfest Park, which now has a new swimming pool, twin shelter houses, three baseball diamonds, a soccer field, a playground and restrooms.

Dusty Woehrmyer and Jeff Thobe take a break between rounds at the New Bremen Rod and Gun Club League Trap Shoot.

*Left:* Bill Woehrmyer of the New Bremen Rod & Gun Club, and Jake, who Woehrmyer unhesitatingly affirms is one good dog.
*Top right:* Mike Springer, Ed Broyles and Mike Glover take their best shot at the League Trap Shoot.
*Bottom right:* Mike Glover, Mike Springer, and Tom Lanskey check the scores at the Rod and Gun Club.

*Left:* Ned Wibbeler takes a break at the Rod and Gun Club.
*Top right:* Tom Lynskey readies for his shot at the League Trap Shoot.
*Bottom right:* Spent shells pile up at the competition.

St. Mary's contingent during a break at the League Trap Shoot. [left to right] Tom Lynskey, Mike Springer, Ed Broyles, Ned Wibbeler, Mike Glover.

GERMAN T
FIRE DEP

$\mathcal{V}$olunteerism instructs the young, builds parks and provides much of how the community protects itself — including the New Bremen Fire Department and the New Bremen Emergency Squad.  Each squad is carried through the years by a cadre of members whose service spans decades. For the fire squad, for example, that group includes Robert Kuck, Sr., who served three decades with the department, including 21 years as chief.



There is no moment so public-spirited, Kurt Vonnegut wrote, as when a fire alarm sounds, setting a volunteer crew into action. In New Bremen, that crew, currently thirty-strong, is under the direction of Fire Chief Bob Kuck, Jr.

By general consent, Kuck said, when you start out as a fireman you don't know much.  The state mandates training for rookies, but experience takes over.  Each fire is different: car, grass, house, silo, machinery, hazardous chemicals — gasoline, ammonia, pesticides.  Some burn, some melt, some smoke is toxic.  What caused the fire? What started it? Look to the smoke while pulling in to the fire scene.  White smoke means wood; black smoke means a synthetic; green smoke means a chemical.

"Through experience you learn how fire acts," Kuck said.  "One of my first fires was at the old Crown Controls.  Fire had burnt through the wooden floor.  The windows were breathing — flexing in and out with the heat.  I was looking for an explosion.  You didn't get one.  Wood burns at a certain degree; it doesn't explode."

Kuck planned to serve five years as chief.  He kept postponing retiring until some task in hand was complete.  In the end, he served 21 years.  "We had a good village council.  A good trustee board.  A good crew.  Didn't have problems with daily bitching — if you had to fight every day for everything, I'd have been out of there a long time ago."

"Almost everything has changed," he added.  "Smoke masks, for instance.  Years ago, an overstuffed chair was made of cotton and wood; pillows were feathers.  Not toxic like foam rubber is today.  Old masks were nothing but a charcoal filter; took the smoke out of the air.  Now, self-contained breathing apparatus on your back and you're breathing from a tank.  Still, pumps still pump water."

Currently, the squad has a 30-member crew.  Its equipment — half a dozen pieces that range from a 1974 4,000-gallon tanker to a 1991 Pierce-Arrow 2,000 gallon-a-minute pumper — is paid for by the village and township.  Chief since 1994 is Robert Kuck, Jr.  "Dad got me involved," he said.  "Now, my son is helping me.  Someone's got to do it.  It's my way of helping the community."  The squad makes about one run a week — 51 through late-December.  The largest number, 19, was to the scene of automotive accidents.  Anytime the emergency squad is called to a car accident, the fire squad rolls; conversely, the emergency squad covers all structure fires.

November 1999 was slow time for the New Bremen Emergency Squad.  Only four runs all month.  "When you go a week, or several weeks without a run," said Bill Young, paramedic and squad member since 1976, "you get the sense that we're due. You have a sensation that the pager is about to go off, and a minute later it does."

In the first four days of December, pagers sounded nine times. Four of these runs involved fatalities — a truck knocked a disabled passenger car into a ditch on Route 66 south of 219, leaving one person dead. The other three died of cerebral hemorrhage, cardiac arrest and a brain aneurysm.

"You don't get used to it," said paramedic Terry Dick. "It's a fact of life. You're going to have people die whatever you do." If a series of runs proves sufficiently distressing, the squad calls in a regional Critical Incident Stress team to de-brief its members. That service, Dick said, "has helped keep a lot of members from bailing out; kept quite a few on the squad."

Retaining members is a high priority, because recruiting new ones is difficult. The year-end 1999 total was the lowest in memory, 21, including six paramedics. Squad work is time consuming. At minimum, members are on call 84 hours a month, plus training. Across Ohio, emergency squads suffer the effects of affluence. A populace with more money at its fingertips and less time on its hands is more willing to support an emergency service with tax dollars than through its own volunteering.

At founding, the squad raised $60,000 to purchase a used ambulance and begin training. The ambulance was stored in the town barn, the training occurred in the high school biology room. Over three decades and it has yet to receive a dime in local tax support. Today, their annual budget is $57,000. Dick estimated that a fully-staffed paid department could cost $1 million.

The work is personal, and immediate. "Most calls are for people we know, or friends of the families," one squad member commented. A second added, "You're always nervous. You never know what you're getting into. Get called for somebody passing out. Get there — pulse is 40 or less; severe heart problem — you load 'em up and take 'em in." Demeanor is important, "If you're excited, don't show it."

The vehicle they load emergency cases into is a mid-1990s Horton ambulance, purchased for $105,000 and thought to have a half dozen years of useful life yet. Inside, the equipment carried shows the breadth of the squad's expertise: a heart monitor that can send EKG reports to the hospital while in transit; a cell phone that connects to a fax machine; equipment to check oxygen/blood levels; a defibrillator to jerk a quivering heart back into normal rhythm.

The squad's own emergency — its need for more members — is a continuing one and one it has thus far managed to surmount. Bill Young said, "About every five years, people say we won't have enough volunteers. Five years pass and we're still going strong."

Beverly Poppe became a Girl Scout volunteer the same day her oldest daughter joined the Brownies. Now, 34 years later, she is in her third term as president of the Girl Scout Council of Appleseed Ridge, covering ten Ohio counties. As a local leader, "I get to watch the girls grow to be citizens that a community can be proud of."

*Top:* Mike "Skinny" Tontrup (left), Robert "Bo" Wissman (center) and Andy Fledderjohann (right) join the town firemen to scrub up the equipment.
*Bottom:* Fire gear at the ready. New Bremen Fire Department.

The Buckeye Hustlers 4-H Club volunteers break for a photo. Fried chicken dinner at St. Paul United Church of Christ. Drive up, pick up, pay and go.

In 1996 and for years previous, all New Bremen school students attended class in a single building, landlocked at the corner of Walnut and Plum streets. While enrollment growth was unspectacular — about two percent a year — that growth, continuing for a decade, pressed on the building's limits.

Trudy Kuenning — a career educator whose own schooling began in the building she now serves as principal — surrounded by New Bremen kindergarteners just starting their own educations. Students are [top row] Liz Fleck, Gregory Finkerbine, Jessie Rindler, Tyler Nosek, [middle row] Brook Thornsberry, Jeff Kuenning, Jarad Gilberg, Doug Kremer, Travis Homan, Taylor Brandts-Carter, Brandon Meyer, Cody Wendel, Tara Nosek [front row] Richael Wynk, Brittany Sayre, Brent Bertke, Gina Griesdorn, Allison Bowers.

The school board consensus was to build a new high school. The question was where. One resident observed, "Many wanted to put the new high school right by the old one." In the end, space may have decided the question. No additional land was available near the existing campus, while the Crown Equipment Corporation offered a 40-acre site on Route 274 one mile east of the downtown.

School board member Dr. James Luedeke said, "We didn't know how it would fly. We set up a levy committee. Got our facts together. Held several public meetings. Drew 300 people to a meeting in the old gym. Presented charts and graphs and the architects. Discussed various options. I thought, we can't leave without taking a straw vote. I asked for show of hands. Based on what you've heard tonight, I said, would you support this. Only about five were opposed."

New Bremen has a history of support for education. Lois Moeller, a long-time New Bremen resident, said, "I don't have a relative here who would vote down a school tax. They all say, 'I figure we were provided a good education by somebody; time for us to do the same.'" The fall 1996 levy was different.

Different, first, because the requested 8.86 mill increase was the largest ever sought. Different, second, because the planned move of the high school from its location since 1929 was, to some, unsettling.

The 15-member levy committee was co-chaired by Mike Brockman and Lori Winner, who had co-chaired a previous successful levy campaign. "When I was asked," Winner said, "I knew how to do it. I'm not afraid to ask people for help. I'm not afraid to humble myself, to tell someone I needed their help because I didn't know how to do something."

The techniques were those of grassroots campaigning. Funds were raised to run ads in the St. Marys and Sidney newspapers. A welcome public endorsement came from the pastor of St. Paul's United Church of Christ. Five hundred window and lawn signs were donated by Crown. The placing around town of 'Apple Trees' — four-foot high laminated cardboard trees bearing 'apples' — were signed by residents as a show of support. "Mostly," Winner said, "it was a matter of getting the information out. I think the most telling argument was the notion that our students would be put at a disadvantage if we didn't build the new school."

Winner, throughout, was confident of success, a confidence many did not share. "I thought all along it would pass. In fact, I thought it would pass by more than it did."

The tally was: Yes: 1045; No: 904.

The school built with the funds the levy made available was dedicated on August 22, 1999. Winner commented, "Even people who voted against the levy, they look at the new complex and are very proud."

And have reason to be. The New Bremen High School must be one of the finest small high schools in the state. In early November, Superintendent Dr. James Roeth provided a tour. The new high school offers room to settle out. Its 99,000 square feet about doubles what the four upper grades shared in the previous location. Everything from chairs to desks to the 90 computers was purchased new for the building. New, too, is the 2100-seat gymnasium. Curiously, it is a gymnasium that has never known defeat.

That will, of course, be put to the test. On December 8, a crowd of 1,800 pushed its way into the gym for the boys' basketball opener. Earlier that day, a student went up to one of the varsity players and said, "New Bremen has never lost in that gym." This statement is true because the previous weekend, the New Bremen Lady Cardinals claimed the Cardinal Tip-Off Tournament with easy back-to-back victories over Anna and New Knoxville. The girls' team has height — three players standing 6-foot or more — and scorers in Jill Buschur and Kate Moeller, who combined for 79 points in the tourney.

The boys' team, too, is tall. Justin Luedeke and Mark Killian both stand 6-foot-7, and neither is willowy. Against New Knoxville, New Bremen uses its height to advantage. The Cardinals are not particularly quick, but quicker to the ball. New Bremen had the ball with thirty seconds left in the first half. A pass. A pass. Another pass. As the clock ticked past ten seconds the crowd became impatient. Another pass. And another pass. With spectators all but climbing out of their seats to get the ball and do *something* with it, senior Mitch Nelson launched a three-pointer as the buzzer sounds. It swished. New Bremen took a 36-25 lead into the break and is not threatened thereafter. The gym remained undefeated for at least another week.

Near the gym is the 460-seat James F. Dicke Auditorium, made possible through a $1 million gift from James F. and Eilleen Dicke. At its entrance, a high school girl lip syncs the rock classic, *I'd Gladly Take You Back.* [And tempt the hand of fate?] Inside, a row of seats contained students mixed with parents. One, in deference to the unseasonable November weather, is wearing khaki shorts. Beyond them, a high ceiling and generous stage, where the auditorium's first production is being presented.

The play is *Rebel Without A Cause,* best known for James Dean's performance in the 1950s movie version. In the local production, Dean's role as Jim Stark is well handled by Greg Moeller, teamed with Erica Lampert as Judy Brown, the girl of his intentions. It is not a play that presents the older generation to advantage. The young people in it, confused and urgent, demand but do not get answers from ineffectual, squabbling parents. It's a teen's view of adults as  useless. Even the local police chief is on the parents' case: "What a way to raise a kid: give them everything he wants and nothing that he needs."

This is not exactly how the visitor imagines life in New Bremen. Nor, said the play's director, Barbara Seiter-Salute, is it particularly how the student cast sees its own lives. "Rebel" was chosen, she said, out of students' wish to open the new auditorium with something serious and well known. They "liked the play's atmosphere. It smacked of rebelliousness, but they're acting. They don't have much experience with rebelliousness, but they do have experience with isolation, loneliness, with not fitting in to a group."

Past the gym, the school offers three large areas. The first is for shop. The second is for vocational agriculture. A quarter of the students have farm backgrounds and Future Farmers of America is the second most popular student activity. The third space is reserved for the school's most popular activity, band. The room is large enough to contain all 105 members of band director Randy Clark's group. The room's mezzanine displays the over 100 awards the band has won — including its recent and first ever Grand Champion award. The room prompted the overheard comment that made Clark's day. "Why is the band room so big and the weight room so small?"

The superintendent's tour passed the remaining classrooms, ducked through a library that offers a large window's clean view of German Township farmland, and ended at the front door. The superintendent is asked if he is now the envy of other superintendents in the area.

He smiled, and replied, "Yes, I am."

Considering the 1999-2000 school year, school board member Dr. James Luedeke gave the district's goals as "good schools, good teachers, good discipline, kids with good study habits, responsive to teachers, with high attendance and low dropout rate." Most school districts could announce these as goals; in New Bremen they are within the district's reasonable grasp.

In recent years, the district has had a 100 percent graduation rate — no dropouts. About three-quarters of its graduates go on to four-year college or technical training. Twice in the past fifteen years, the district has been named a Hall of Fame school and, during 1998-1999, scored 18 out of 18 in the state Department of Education review.

Contrast those results against another figure. During the 1998-1999 school year, per pupil expenditure in the New Bremen schools was $5,378 — a full 20 percent below the statewide average of $6,754. Asked for comment on this ratio of achievement to expenditure, school superintendent Roeth said, with some fairness, that his district "is doing the best with the dollars the community gives us." He added, "You will find that this is generally true in Auglaize County. It's a lot of things. The high expectations that schools and parents set. The fact that attendance is high" — it averages 96.4 percent — "so the kids are here in the school everyday."

There is a good fit between teachers and students. Most teachers recruited into the district come from within twenty-five miles of New Bremen and share its values. The teaching staff is stable, averaging eighteen years in the classroom, most of those years in New Bremen. Teachers who come, stay. "When I interviewed here," said band director Clark, "it wasn't my intention to stay. I thought, 'It's a jumping stone, I'll be here five years, then move on.' But it proved too nice to leave." There is, said fourth grade teacher Becky Keller, "a strong community *inside* the school."

Fourth grade teacher Darlene Gilberg said, "I fell into this post. Now that I'm here, I love it. I love the kids. They want to care for you. The sense of humor is there. They still have their innocence." High points of the year, she said, were presenting the musical *Stone Soup* and a trip to the Sunwatch reconstructed Indian village near Dayton. The low point was "taking the fourth grade proficiency exam. It was their first experience with standardized tests." The proficiency exams, which the state requires at various grade levels, showed high results. In 1998-1999, 92 percent of fourth-graders passed in reading: 94 percent in math; 95 percent in citizenship; 89 percent in science; 82 percent in writing.

The opening of the new high school put 310 students in the new building, left 680 in the old one. With the move, Trudy Kuenning — longtime K-6 principal — became principal for K-8. "They say I'm going to be chaperoning a junior high dance in the gym," she said. "The last time I attended a junior high dance in that gym, I had a date."

*Top left and right:* The playing fields of New Bremen High School, where — depending on the season — the Cardinals either roll to the goal or round third, heading for home.

*Bottom left:* Painted in the gym of the old high school, this cardinal — the school's symbol — suggests a message suitable for rivals: 'Don't Tread on Me.'

*Bottom right:* A New Bremen pole vaulter, a red crescent, clears the bar at the excellent new athletic facility on State Route 274. The old high school track was not regulation in length; it ran near a pasture, and cows mooed at runners as they passed by. For these reasons, track meets were generally held away.

*Left:* Fourth grade teachers Darlene Gilberg and Becky Keller and an accumulation of the books their students grow up on.

*Top right:* Elementary school students streak east to west across a painted playground map of the United States.

*Bottom right:* The ever fresh artwork of students. When children render the world, they fill it with a race of characters with large faces and insignificant bodies, like these painted by students at the New Bremen Elementary School. They do so, perhaps, because it is the expression on the face that tells them what they most need to know.

Lessons in territoriality. *Left:* Schoolgirls hold a visiting photographer at bay. *Top right:* First-grade chums Sarah Kaiser, Emily Topp, Taylor Schmit and Lindsay Ahrns hold the line. *Bottom right:* Elementary school students rally near the jungle gym.

*Top left:* The local 'Music Man,' Randy Clark, and a quartet of students playing French horns, many feet of coiled brass, from which a mellow, woodland sound emerges. For Clark, music is about more than making a sound; it is also about making a difference. "If we at the high school don't expose the kids to culture and the arts, then it won't happen. It's up to us to see they aim higher." In the background, a smattering of the awards the school band has won.

*Top right:* Getting the day started, a student runs to catch up with the morning bus.

*Bottom left:* With school grounds just across the street, progress slows to a decent walk.

*Bottom right:* The scorers box of the old high school, where the score keepers hung out.

Through a baritone brightly. An arc of cornetists make music with three valves and a certain amount of lip. Cornets and clarinets tend to have more players than do trombones, which are expensive, ungainly, and quite simply difficult to play.

$\mathcal{I}$t is in the young that the changes in the world register with their elders.  Mary Ahlers commented, "We feel so completely different than our children.  So much more is offered to them than was offered to us.  I was the first of my cousins to leave Toledo.  Now, three-quarters of those who leave for college don't come back."

College is the watershed. Those presented with a larger world often chose to remain in it. Lois Moeller said, "All of my son's best friends have scattered."

Change mounts upon change. New Bremen was an agricultural town until the early 1960s. It became industrial then. Businesses had been oriented to agriculture. The hardware store sold farm things. Groceries had meat lockers in the back so farmers could bring a steer in for slaughter, then keep the meat in the locker. That way, farms didn't need a freezer.

New Bremen is changing, again. It is new, or old, depending on where one looks. Drive down Franklin Street, or Herman, or Plum and it's a well-kept small Ohio town. Drive through the Pioneer subdivision or past the new high school on Route 274 and the setting is new, upscale and vaguely suburban. Mary Ahlers noted a symptom of that change. "Before, we had the [Hollingsworth] Hotel; now we've got the Grille. It's a loss and a gain. The hotel has so many memories of birthday parties. The bar side and the other side. When you were old enough, you graduated to the bar side. Now, it's so reserved."

Another example. The New Bremen Coffee Co. & Books Inc. opened on Monroe Street. It is an enterprise that, by wares and origin, would not have been found in New Bremen a decade ago. It sells books, upscale coffees and locally baked desserts and grew out of the excess energy of a local book club, all of whose members were women, as are the store's organizers. One, Susan Heitkamp, said, "We've been very pleased with the response. Both from white collar people and from kids on their way to school. You have to explain to them that cappuccino is not something you get in a can or out of a machine." Such explanations are an incremental contribution to the sophistication of the local young.

New Bremen is growing. Dentist Ron Riebel puts this as aptly as any. "Once, three cars at the light was a traffic jam; now, it can actually happen that you don't get through the intersection on the next cycle."

Quasi-officially, New Bremen favors growth.

Mayor Robert Klein says, "The current rate of growth is good. If it wasn't, we couldn't be a community. We'd become stagnant without at least a bit of change."

Village manager Tony Bales adds, "Bigger? We don't want to sit still. We don't want the world to pass us by."

Notions abound. The Community Improvement Corporation wants new industry in town. Mayor Klein thinks the old swimming pool might make the starting point for an amphitheater. Daryl Dammeyer believes the old canalway ought to be developed with small shops.

Still, there is hesitancy. Ginny Winner, of Hair Performers, said, "I want New Bremen to grow, but not at the expense of drug problems like Sidney or gangs like Celina." Darlene Gilberg, fourth grade teacher, added, "I'd like New Bremen to slow down on building. I came to a quaint small environment; don't want it to become too big. Being from a larger place, I want to keep it small." Mary Ahlers said, "Even as large as St. Marys, you lose the quaintness."

"I like New Bremen," said Bryan Trego, proprietor of Bolly's. "I like the changes. I know it's good to have the mall. But I also like the old Bremen. When Rax opened up, people would say, 'Hey, great, we've got fast food.' But pretty soon it became a place to go just if you wanted to eat quick."

Officials acknowledge the contradiction. Mayor Klein says, "We don't want New Bremen to become a city." At 5,000, an Ohio place becomes a city, a change with legal and, likely, psychological consequences. Manager Bales thinks, "We want to grow, without being changed by growth."

Some see growth, for small towns, as a pact with the devil. Or, Biblically more accurate, perhaps, as akin to Esau, trading one's birthright for a K-Mart and an expanding tourist trade. For growth to be something that New Bremen can direct, two things must hold: first, its economy must remain strong; second, others must view it as attractive. In short, New Bremen must be a seller's market.

"In today's market," said Greg Myers, executive director of the Southwestern Auglaize County Chamber of Commerce, "I don't think there's anything that's bankable." Meaning, there is no certain formula for success. Within the Chamber, he said, job creation is not the first priority. "If this were a less prosperous area, it would be. We're fortunate to have the number of industrial jobs that we do. Instead, we're looking for diversity. We're looking for anything that is a cutting edge technology; information industry." To lure such business, "We are selling quality of life. Kids are safe here. You know your neighbors. You don't have to lock your car every time you run into a store. As the world becomes more anxious over these things, this place becomes more attractive." And, Myers said, as technology makes it easier for skilled people to work where they wish, that wish is likelier to bring them here. Thought through, what this means is that New Bremen will be sustained economically by that which makes it attractive as a place to live.

Economic strategies are pursued, successfully or not, by the few. The broader public may take an interest, but generally does not engage. Engagement reflects where the community puts its energy. Asked what rallies New Bremen, the largest number reply: its schools. Fr. Conlon stated, "Building the new high school. It's a source of pride, an indication of prosperity, of the community's ability to work together, its willingness to pay taxes." Daryl Dammeyer commented, "The town is very school-oriented. It gets behind sports, the band. It rallies behind the church." The Rev. Tostrick noted "the schools" and added, "There's the urge to care for the community, like you find in the fire and emergency squads. A giving attitude." What you don't do, is largely the converse.

"The local 'No-no?'" Dammeyer responds. "Talking bad about the schools. That's like talking against someone's church, which you also don't do." In New Bremen, said Fr. Conlon, "The worst thing you can do is 'dis' New Bremen."

**Top left:** Corn stalks trimmed of silage. German Township fields bring forth abundantly. In a county that averages 120 bushels of corn to the acre, German Township routinely brings forth 150.

**Bottom left:** Windmills reached Europe in the 12th century; they reached Ohio with settlement. This windmill on the Stauffer farm on Clover Four Road is typically American, a high, lightweight tower and concave vanes, kept facing the wind by a tail geared to a shaft.

**Right:** The crystal sunlight of winter casts this detailed shadow of the fence near the Queen Anne house at the Crown Farm.

***Top left:*** German Township herds decline in size, yet total milk production continues to grow. Local cows take this news, like all news, placidly.

***Top right:*** Make it through winter, you'll make it to fall. True not just of people, but of buildings, as well. These farm buildings on Route 66, having managed the hard months, show up to re-enlist for one more spring.

***Bottom left:*** View of spring corn along Amsterdam Road.

***Bottom right:*** Field along Lock Two Road creates extemporaneous beauty, where purple hen bit and alfalfa precede the plow.

***Opposite:*** West of New Bremen. Glowing as it brushes through a line of trees, the sun departs New Bremen as it has done 60,000 times previously.

Two men and a muse. Writer Mark Bernstein (left) and photographer Bob Flischel in a brief respite. For six months, they combined a plethora of their talents to discover, document, and distill a town that, in return, rewarded them with openness, friendship, and quietude — an artist's nirvana.